Limes and Compromise

poems by

Erika Saunders

Finishing Line Press
Georgetown, Kentucky

Limes and Compromise

*For my family: Chris, Jacob, Seija and Elizabeth.
With all my love.*

Copyright © 2019 by Erika Saunders
ISBN 978-1-63534-883-5 First Edition
All rights reserved under International and Pan-American Copyright Conventions.
No part of this book may be reproduced in any manner whatsoever without written permission from the publisher, except in the case of brief quotations embodied in critical articles and reviews.

ACKNOWLEDGMENTS

Thank you to all of the journals and editors for publishing the following poems:

Cholla Needles: "Desert Sun Desiccation," "Firescapes at Burdick Cabin," "Recipe for Baked Hippopotamus," "Surviving on Limes and Compromise," "Viperfish"
Midwest Apocalypse: "It Begins Quiet as a Side-Look Stare"
Oakwood Literary Magazine: "Blind Hope," "Feast," "Whiteout"
Pasque Petals: "All a-Winter-ling," "Autumn Homecoming," "Baked Hippopotamus," "Clarity Leaving Blues," "Crossroad of Bones," "Crows," "Cryptomeria," "Elephant Charge," "Fused Salt"
Pensées Intimes Magazine: "Tastefully Attired"
Red Wheelbarrow Literary Magazine: "Poppy Preserve, May 1994"

Publisher: Leah Maines
Editor: Christen Kincaid
Cover Art: Jessie Rasche (www.jessierasche.com)
Author Photo: Christopher Saunders
Cover Design: Leah Huete; Hitch Studio (www.hitchstudio.com)

Printed in the USA on acid-free paper.
Order online: www.finishinglinepress.com
        also available on amazon.com

Author inquiries and mail orders:
Finishing Line Press
P. O. Box 1626
Georgetown, Kentucky 40324
U. S. A.

Table of Contents

Poppy Preserve, May 1994 1

Desert Sun Desiccation 2

Clarity Leaving Blues 4

Fused Salt 5

Tastefully Attired 6

Viperfish 7

Recipe for Baked Hippopotamus 8

Feast 9

Crossroad of Bones 10

Crows 11

Waving as You Pull Out of the Driveway 12

Baked Hippopotamus 14

Elephant Charge 16

Electric Monsoon Season: Encounters Along the
    Nä Pali Coast 18

Surviving on Limes and Compromise 21

Cryptomeria 22

Autumn Homecoming 24

Whiteout 25

All a-Winter-ling 26

Firescapes at Burdick Cabin 28

Blind Hope 32

It Begins Quiet as a Side-look Stare 34

Poppy Preserve, May 1994

Lovely these droughted, bone-
bleached seeds. Wind scattered
along sandy valley floors, parched
remnants of yesteryear—sowed.

Rains release, set-off a petal
painful burst—unfurling symmetry
in spades. A super bloom of fields
swathed in burnt sunshine. A girl

strolls through this radiant glow,
striking like the sun's coronal loops
and urchin roe. She sidesteps
the regal owl's clover and lupine;

the false flash in the pan
of goldfield, cream cups
and coreopsis—to pick a poppy
and tuck it behind her ear.

The plucked poppy folds
in an *abhaya mudra*, murmuring
a peaceful prayer farewell
to the wind-faced sway, to the heat

melting mirage of titian swirling,
green strands twinning, where pollen drops
stroke pollen drops as gentle as coral
marine polyps blushing; such uprooted grace,

a pilgrim now, striking forth
from this seething mass of gold.

Desert Sun Desiccation

The desert sun desiccates vaporous forms; mists transpire.

I met a boy once out there leaning
against a wall all a serious stare. New
to town. The eyes, the-eyes, the-yes,
these-eyes bore into me past budding
breasts and simple hips, to the core
unhiding the fear of it all. And fear
meets fear meets love.

In the desert where things go to die—sun spots
flash across surreal shadows—and our generation like that.

He looked at me and I saw myself. Petty
and trite using my long legs and lean
lies to kill the boredom of life in the desert
as artificial as the aqueduct dribble, trickle
of the false river, a mermaid's beard, all
entombed in concrete. I went feral that year
for virgin lips are heavy to the touch.

Scorched desert strangle-hold days and then the wind
blows embedding sand like pepper spray.

How love? When I only wanted
to know just enough to know his
story matched mine. Lives of shifting
sand, where fathers skipped mothers
who skipped daughters and sons down
the road, sand-shrivelled dreams
indecorously exposed.

The tumbleweeds hasten along desperate to escape
the parched lips thirst-lust-sand scrambling atop one another.

Watching them pinned in by the chain
link fence, how they build a fire squad
pail brigade seemingly horizontal. Clinging
one-on-one with thorny fingers, craggy
claws. Desperate to blow free, desperate
to cling to their thorny embrace—and
the apex is love.

Clarity Leaving Blues

Wishing on the blue but taking what I can
get; high density foam and the kite festival all
in a pink pickled herring. Stranger neighbors
nod their hellos as the ocean tosses in the air;

sailing whales and plump-faced octopi dock
to fields of wonder zigzagged by knock-kneed
old men who admire the youth—Chagrin!
Watching the green haze clarity leaving blues

and you, while Marrimekko black and white
dots the sun. If only I had thrusters that roared
in your ears, I'd lift you into my air with flared
lips and challenging eyes, whisking you along

star trails and cosmic dust-ways. I'd deposit
you at the footsteps of the pillars of creation
to bear witness to the maelstrom of star birth
and gamma ray bursts as black hole gravities

collide. I'd pluck you a bouquet of swirling
rose galaxies mixed with pearl star-drop baby's
breath as we dine on crab nebulas and dance
along the wispy remains of nova explosions;

you would acquiesce to a kiss, fusing our two
billowing lobes of gas and dust into a titanic supernova
fulminating so vehemently our surroundings would
collapse under the gravity of us: a galaxy new-born.

If only, as you saunter by with the breeze in
your eyes and the sun to your back, and I turn
to find the wine has grown warm in my flask.

Fused Salt

Out at the farmhouse,
she was hanging clothes on the line

> *a molten salt reactor*
> *stays at low vaporous pressure*

in her cut-off jean shorts with
chestnut hair that captures sun-flares.

> *with nuclear fission—*
> *the primary coolant,*

As she turns and looks up and down
this California sunshine soldier-man

> *or even the fuel itself,*
> *is a molten salt mixture;*

walking up the drive; and bites her lip-

> *use sparingly.*

Tastefully Attired

Just as Arctic explorers wear
synthetics to protect against the wet-
cold, I too wore all synthetics with flare:

faux leather shorts, fishnet stockings,
four-inch wedges and that slinky,
violet tank. The day, daydreaming

I was hopscotching crevasses or perhaps
licking molasses, I walked into you in the hall.
With black eyeliner blazing like pinball

stripes against lids the shade of electric
blue guitars I winked and pinned you against
the wall, kissing you long and hard. You tasted

of caviar. That night, with your legs paperclipped
to mine we heaved, churned, and buckled like trolley
cars derailed. Caught as we were in the moon-pull,

tide-lure (grasp-release) salty moonshine. As
dawn broke like diamond lust I lingered by your
side dressed in the pink-tongued morning light.

Viperfish

You watch me, quiet, with eyes
vacant as a polynya
while you light a cigarette
and sip your coffee,
stale. It's true

I am suspicious of your
intentions since any redeeming
qualities seem scarce, yet
those lips, that chest. So,
I dive. Into you, drawn

down into the depths
by your viper-like flash
of phosphorescence.
I dive. Like all other organic
detritus, joining

with the dead or dying plankton,
protists, sand, and soot
floating down becoming,
bit by bit, the marine snow
you'll feed on.

What is left for us
to say? The hypnotic shine
of your bioluminescence
so beautiful, I dive,
compressed by

the pressure, knowing
you'll devour me whole. Yet,
I dive so deep it no longer
matters, for if I were to surface
now—I'd explode.

Recipe for Baked Hippopotamus

You tell me your plan to bake the
hippopotamus binding it in banana
leaves salted and spiced with Jamaican

coffee, second day leftover grounds
need not go to waste. To lower him
whole by the gold leash braided. Lost

time because while you can blanket and
spice, never could you slice clean slivers of
time—red ribboning out-veining the blue

of space tucked into the earth. This
earth dug extensively by ancestors,
women sure enough of you and me

and meeting and walking hands entwined
and staying still after you spilled your salted
staleness breath against my neck, to dig—

to dig, and dig out the prairie blue clay
turned to red carved pipes. As the grandfathers
sit around the pit edge smoking prayers

to you to go, keep going—not to be tricked
by the star singing fox into the bear
baiting old woman's tear streaked face-hole.

Feast

Summer came through water rush
spring rivers, tributaries grown
salty with Asian carp zingers, swatted

this way and up; heaven shoots
bambooing to God's prayer hands
woven into parachutes of miniscule

time. Bits of bread salted, stale, long arms
wide smile, vanishing point assured you bow
your head and say, "Feast!" But laid bare

long and low across the white tablecloth
dotted with oil-black coffee stains and Saltine
crumbles (served freely every Friday

afternoon at the Union Hall) I see nothing
but carcasses floating face up; brother
and mother and daughter all cheeks shining

salted tears. Wearing crowns of
clouds where water-meets-sky-meets
their closed eyes, closed lips cracked

as music across time, their grief hearts
turning slowly over silver encrusted spits like
the flesh of you all this time crocked, set to

bake slowly near the warm banked
coals of a lifetime of endless askance.

Crossroad of Bones

Our arms a crossroad of bones
at 3am when I wake rolling
to hold you. You shift and
settle, I think back to the pickaxe
weight while digging out
corpses encased in mud—
packed coffins washed
ashore, a ship wreck. All
women and children pale
and bloated and dirt
smeared. Wondering how I
could be both digging and
entombed, I turn only to toss
my mind, wiggling nearer
again, back to back; as if
awaiting a gun fight. Legs
cast along sheets of distance
between us, growing; as
tomorrow I will get up and help
you pack to fly to Denver to
talk renewable energy, and;
I don't know, maybe get
high with a little help
from your friends. As

I rise to find pen and paper
you sense my leaving, sleep reach
cradle me in the crook of your arm,
gently cupping my breast.

Crows

Perched delinquents—a feathery gang
preening blue-black, chest plump,
eyes waterless-wells—gaze out along bared, bicep—

curled branches appointing time.
Roosting among Valley Oaks bearded in
Spanish moss. Crows sit to call insults branch by

branch, and then (once noticed) to spit
them down on me. Laughing I shrug, tugging
your hand we elephant along the hill—

crest. Tilting left, Little Valley with its winding dust
roads that embank crumbling brittle-grassed
meadows; tilting right, Round Valley with far reaching

grids demarcating Crocus and Indian
Soldiers who bloom, seed, and die, again, again.
Exposed up there like bare legs on ice,

the summer sun noon begins to bake my
lips—mimicking the cracked earth. Scabbed
remains-where spring puddles pocked

beneath the silky dust. We forget them in
the heat-haze waving, oiled-air mirage
that dances under my raised sun-capped

hand, blurring their black dot aero-motion.
Swooping wing beats breeze above, fans premonition.
You throw rocks yelling affronts, which register

return nothing but indifferent air, shadows trail
caw mocks caw mocks caw, declares
they're settling in for the bone picking wait.

Waving as You Pull Out of the Driveway

When you leave,
    you untether me—
        floating
on an inland sea.
    Like all hollow vessels,
        I bob on the tide; dipping
in and out of this alkali
    cocktail—dipping
        and drying like wax
to wick, which tans my skin
    to crack-lin.
        In the dead-soft inland
sea, I float facing the cloudless
    sky—palms spread,
        sun-kissed as Santiago's
as he's washed onto
    the beachhead. Ox
        peckers descend,
settling onto my blistering
    breast, they pass over my sea-
        lice friends
to blood-let the host
    instead. I bleed
        in salted cracker-crust
white, and my eyes
    blink as hollow
        as Iamus
before his descent.
    Suspended
        in this saturated

salinity—fuchsia dreams
      erupt like Matisse cut-outs
            and drift along beside
me in the brine
      shrimp bloom. Where I think
            I see you along the shore,
smeared in red heifer ash,
      caught mid-dive, and I await
            your purifying splash.

Baked Hippopotamus

I told you all along it was a bad
idea to take the hippo through the
house. He was too big and knowing he

was to be a carcass wrapped in
cellophane tossed after two weeks
anyway, he chose to obstinately

stand. It would have been better for
us all (and by that, I mean less bother and
imposition on me and mine) had

you just grabbed his leash and pretended
to take him for a walk out the front, down
the side path, turning at the corner of

universal time and space and dusty
trails that lead nowhere; out back to
the old woman. Who, digging with tears

and wails, cements mud bricks to line
the walls of a hollowed-out oven sized
enough to bake a hippo whole. But

through the house you went, so here we
all are at the kitchen counter where you hold
loose his leash of gold and pearl—dainty,

like a revolver—dainty, like your fine hands
smoothed and white that pray to me in
the night. Stroking my hair and thighs and lips

begging them to part and yet pressed to salty
silence. We all sit here filling space with a hippo
we cannot eat though feeding him will do us all

in. I pull out a crockpot and begin chopping
onions and carrots and celery for we are suddenly
French, and I will salt then sweat them before

tossing knuckles and shoulders of pork in; while
the old woman out back rages for the cosmic
time she wasted digging that hole.

Elephant Charge

He came trumpeting in through the windows
catching me unawares as I scrubbed day old egg
crust off the bottom of the cast iron pan. Noisy,

once spotted, found in every window, a glimpsed
waving ear here, and fingering snout there; walking
along the walls. Suddenly grown sneaky silent.

Exasperated, I went down to the storage closet, to
get the hippo I had laid away, had heaved onto the top
shelf, for just such an occasion. "I'll show you, you pesky

son of a bitch." thinking, "You can't steal my circus
peanuts anyway!" and with a grunt braced my knees.
Lugged the old thing down (much like the blue Samsonite

my aunt lent me a decade ago; that I can't figure
out if I should return or use or give to Goodwill) and
sat it down by the front door.

Drawing all the blinds to create a dayglow, warm
like how the super moon trespassed into my bedroom
midnight sleep-waking for a week, I drew a chair to keep

him company for the wait. Sure enough, just as the air
grew stale, and the conversation waned, there came
a snuffling sound, akin to autumn sweeping

the leaves scrapping along the front step. When and then
and there he suddenly was standing in the vestibule, having
busted down the door, (anyone else would have just knocked)

standing as if a superhero "S" was emblazoned in the air
before him. With confident triumphant grin, I declare, "Get him!"
to the dogs and the hippo and the thin air

but not a one stirred. Looking from eyes, to eyes to air; growing
more exasperated, I declare again; as if they might be Pete in a
boat and need a re-Pete, "Get him!" A dog whined and tamped his

tail along the floorboards, the hippo began cleaning his fingernails
and the air left the room. Turning to chastise them all for
cowardice, zeroing in on the hippo I demand, "Where is it now?

Where that bombastic way just last month you sat
and yelled "Systemic Risk!"? Where now?" but my
mistake, with back exposed the bastard came in for the kill.

And with a smile, began weaving his charms, hands swirling
that "S" rainbowing the air into unicorns and candies and
bullshit, grand wizarding his way further into the room.

Backing the hippo up against the wall, further into the
house cajoling and galumphing, winning my dogs to heel,
(I guess loyalty can be bought) until much to my shagreen, I

find myself sitting next to him on the fading
couch, serving tea and peanuts.

Electric Monsoon Season: Encounters Along the Nä Pali Coast
—In monsoon season there are two options: wait for the rain to pass or trudge on through.

I.   We Stumble upon an Argyria Shaman

A blue-skinned shaman
        stands alone in a day-use-only
                park shelter watching dusk fall
like lavender dust
        in the falling rain storm. He greets us
                with a story of the Mexican Cartel
bulldozing tourist's
        dead bodies by the thousands
                into mass graves. Only pausing
to ask
        if we had brought any
                smokes. Stacked on a cut
tree stump
        an oversized Mexican-silver
                serving tray capture the rainwater.
His fresh water
        source. Thin as communion
                wafers his fingers slip silver rings
etched with intricate inlays
        up and down habitually
                like pistons firing.

II.   Survival Skills

Beluga bones litter the beach
from those left abandoned by
low tide. Beached bears chew on
beluga bones that litter the coast at
low tide. Beach bears chew on
the meat—bone clean. Bare tooth to
beluga bones that litter the coast,
etchings, a tide-licked art form.

III.   The Shaman Describes the Local Flora

And boom! It hits
            you in the face. Third
degree—hotter than
            the sun, is especially
hot for the face
            and genitals. He waves
his hand over
            his crotch and nods
emphatically. All
            of the things
that live on the sun,
            dogs, cats and people—
creatures
            on the surface
of the sun dance
            and consume
themselves
            to give us heat.

IV.   Inventory

Cook pot filled with lemons—
            mangos within reach and a
                        three-day stale high.

V.   The Shaman Teaches Us to Teleport

It helps to begin in warrior pose
he assures us as rain rushes by on
the mud-slick trail. Don't worry,

the toads will save you from going
beyond your limit. They have saved
me several times. Toads are known

to exhibit breeding site fidelity after
all. Remove all batteries near you,
clearing a zone free of electrical

interference. Like fifty feet. Then
you can teleport up to five feet at a time.
It helps if you begin in warrior pose.

VI.   The Shaman Describes Time Spent at a Buddhist Monastery

Lightbulbs kept blowing out before
       their time —
peace be with the electrician who got the call.

He explains, "Being color-blind, I go
       by feel. It's all
from the core, what some might call the soul"

and he concentrates his consciousness
       until all the energy—
electrons and protons, get in line.

Monks claim that peace is in the core of you—
       the soul, I guess.
I don't know if they can eat the light.

Surviving on Limes and Compromise

Lobsters, both
       blue and red,
              with their dissipating
nervous systems
       feel their dying on
              a continuum
like echoes
       along a string.
              While their claws
clamp, claws
       clamp in a primal impulse.
             Grasping at life
with a death-drum
       rhythmic pulse,
              that no amount
of prayer
       and incense can clean
              from your memory.

Cryptomeria

This soul lock love
thunder-moon mix
of hidden snips;

where dreams drift
around us like new—
born dogwood

blossoms, shaken
loose by the sweeping
spring thunderstorm.

Waking, you caress
the warm underside
of worlds
transcribed along
my skin,
a carapace of
cicatrices.

Murmuring "on ne
saurait dire ce quelle
souffeit" as your

fingertips trace,
connecting
constellations,
as graceful as dying
stars.

Slowly unfurling
like ivy
I curl around you
as the impulses
of gravitational
waves
ripple along
the fabric of space-
time.

Clinging
together like two
neutron stars
colliding,
we shower this world
in a fata morgana
of gold.

Autumn Homecoming

Golden spindly cornstalks; lean, bleached, hollowed
husks, light like dried bird bones, flicker out the car

window—an old film reel unwound. Sunlight's running
ray thumbs the silken tassels grown worn as these book

pages, dogeared and fraying. Sunflowers cease their
neck craning, day-long sun stalking to unmask; dark

wizen toothless crones, heads bowed, breasts drooping
and limp-skinned as Rodin's *Old Courtesan*. Sorghum

turns burgundy, fleshy like the western Chinook, run
upstream done; battered and spent delicately floating

in the eddies' gentle repose. Fields flush with Goldenrod
and Sourgrass flit, flaunt, dart by while the Big Sioux crusts;

dressed dazzlingly in a gossamer morning mist; vaporously
bejewelling the willows banking the shore. Winds shake

spent cicada husks from Ashes raining dry and discarded
like so much summer splendour decay. Clouds soldier in,

bulwarking the sun against skies bruised purplish blue
and grey as a jinxed lover, and the geese veer east

as you pull into the drive; where we find our way strewn
with a harvest of maple death masks awaiting the pyre.

Whiteout

In a blizzard it isn't the snow that'll get you but the wind. Gusting to whiteout. An oppressive wind, that will knock you down and plaster-cast you frigidly in place. When I was summer-young and went swimming, I would break the water surface, throwing my head back to toss my long hair. When I didn't use enough force, my hair stayed slicked to my face, an oil spill; I tried to suck breath through that sealed curtain door. And I marvelled at drowning amidst all that air. Blizzard winds will drown you too, suction-cupping snow to your lips, freezing red your nostril tips. It's said, old-timers tied a rope from the house to the barn, navigating by feel alone, trusting that rope in that near-numb, white-blind world. I imagine they heard, on a Sunday, of the priest entering the Holy of Holies with a rope around his ankle, so his dead body could be pulled out if he wasn't worthy. I wonder if those old-timers gave it a thought as they bundled up to go feed the livestock. Maybe they strained thinking they heard those ephod bells a-ringing in the wind. Stories tell of those who lost their grip and froze to death within a few feet of their own front door step. You, my love, resembled the rope.

All a-Winter-ling

How the conscious floating
fall, the gentle descent must
feel,
as the turtles
waffle down to settle
into mud-suckering
shallow holes.

          All a-winter-ling,
like those turtles, I settle to the
bottom of this life; the daily
repetition
of the daily grind. Always
another chore undone, still;

needing me. To survive I allow
myself to go cold, intentionally,
like those turtles. Heart
slowed, mind lulled by
the mind-numbing
repetition
from this day
to that. Not for lack of love,

my love; but instead a
survival instinct. Because only
by slowing the heartbeat, by
relegating the duty of breathing
to the tail can one consciously
keep one's self
stuck
in the mud.

But you grow weary of my
weariness, I know my love.

Count on spring to come
with fits and starts like
the way I work on self-
improvement; intentional
but inconsistent.

                    It often
seems that Spring has
trouble getting her shit
together too.

But I can forgive her more
readily than I can myself,

She has a lot more on her plate.
But even as a hot-mess she

makes it. And I will too. Breaking
free of the freezing mud my

smiling, twinkle heart eyes-
bright love-beat, so like those

ectotherms, will pop to the surface
once more.

Firescapes at Burdick Cabin

I.

A soul blanket of flannel coats
my thoughts as the morning
mountain air distilled through
the screen to a fine chill

accompanies me out the door
to the fire pit littered with
yesterday's memories; half
crushed pop cans lightly

seared. I poke around to find
the embers, the beating heart
of hope among the gray and
bitter ash that washes the face

in a fine coat like a holy pilgrim,
as I begin ritualistically breathing.
Breathing with eyes closed, in slow
deep breaths, keeping time with

the pines gentle synchronized
syncopation. Breathing long and
low and steady as if reviving a long
stilled drum beat echo against the

bald rock face. Breathing with such
purpose as if to blot out the sun
with the simmering smoke sprouts,
that curl the pine needles finely—

like a daughter's hair. Until I am
so full of the moment and the breath
and the ember's growing promise
that I might explode into air myself.

II.

My bones have grown sun-
bleached, dry, light to the touch,
just as these pine branches cut
and left last fall, awaiting the fire.

How they must long all winter
long, blanketed in freeze as they
are and piled haphazardly like
love, for their turn to roast.

My god how I long to go out that way,
to be cast on the flames like passion.

III.

I met you there on the pine branch bough to ride shotgun
through the Wild West prop towns, west past the moonscape
(lunar landing screen stage available for purchase at the pawnshop)
out to the hills.

To the hills where the toaster sprouts Dutch tulips
all in a-yellow and the fire crackles drunk on pine
cones and pizza boxes. Where dreams get stashed, bottled
up blue atop shelves like fireflies in a jar, and the stars call
out your name.

Where, in escape from an imperfect world, we are at home
in soul silence and children's giggling screams of wonder;
hair is left undone and care disappears burned away in
the hot fire's ember glow.

The pines snapchat sunsets and wildling does;
while the lake trout leap like your laughter
in the gentle evenings heart beat ebbing flow of bird's song.

IV.

Gnarly black horseflies
buzz, insisting on movement
and change. To move on.

It is uncomfortable to sit into,
settling on, our imperfections
anyway. To know time seasons

with a heavy hand and can cut
any moment with but a flick
of the wrist. But in the dying

fire light moment who will
be left to tally the cost?

V.

Fire defies the love of
symmetry. Like a new
colt all knock-kneed
and wobbly it stumbles

about flicking away
the pesky flies of change
and time and recklessly
heads on in a gambling gait.

You banked the coals last
night like memories tucked
away in a hope chest, and
sighed away the burdens
that cannot be changed.

VI.

Up through the pine canopy
sifting flour clouds play about;
harassing the blues and greens
until they disguise themselves

in golden. And searching in the yellow
pages I find the ember coaxed back
from extinction like the Dodo could
have been. Fire takes three I decide,

as the lopsided flames renew their lease on life,
and the steaming coffee mimics the love of firescapes.

Blind Hope

To trick the surface of the earth to begin
to believe again, in the smooth turtle

shell pock marks sanded and buffed
and polished; to shine Diana's mirror back

against time and bloat and these small
hands wrapping banana leaves around your

neck, a bull hippo bellowing in rage as
the boat floats the salted crocodile eye-

lights. Smooth, steady hunt the river edged
shallows where bended reeds help

buoy the ridiculous weight of it all. For
you know the years will be danced out

along your back, feet-stepping-feet delicate
carefully, tenderly, lovingly, vertebrae by

vertebrae like my fingertips kissing trace
as you sleep stomach-down, face turned

to the wall, arms elbowing out like
geometry. You know I could climb the rivers

lazily adapting; giggle at being mistaken for
the albino river dolphin and dream

of time, and playing tricks on you in the dusky
blue waters warmed by the cosmic thinning

of space. I could glide silent as an eel into the reed
roots of space and time; while you doze in the deep

heart of night, cock-assured of your place
in the world; to tickle loose the roots of things

like freedom and reason and tie them around
your toes, shoe-stringing you to your desk chair.

It Begins Quiet as a Side-look Stare

When age-life-disease incapacitates
your youthful memories of me, Chinese
takeout and Fred Astaire flicks; magnolias,

older than bees, dance lovingly in the spring
delicate white-hot wind winter remains,
blushing. Gentle as goose down, silent

ashes fall out our kitchen window raining
the magnolias dry, brittle: bottom ash,
fly ash mixed with buffalo hooves, roughing

in a landscape of blues, black and gray. All
those nights we dream-talked away with
John Prine and wine. Agents of change—earth,

wind, soil stripped bare, barbed-wire, fence
posts tilted, unstrung. Sun eclipsed by putrid
clouds, land shrouded in a sifting ash-crust,

thickening city streets and homes into catacombs;
cremains of a world man-spit on a charcoal brazier.
Perhaps the magnolia was never hearty enough—

sunk, numb; I watch your leaving me, footsteps
echoing like hot coals and the crested pigeon screams
with flapping feathered wings. Magnolias shaken,

I awake alone in this atomic town, heart-grief-lost,
to find you: huddled remains entombed, kneeling
in those magnolia ashes a plaster cast Pompeiian

relief; crumbling—touch, I smear this Vibhuti
in three parallel lines waving like water on my pale,
shrinking, favillia skin. All apocalypses are local.

Erika Saunders grew up between her home in California and her grandparent's farm in Indiana. She holds a degree in education from the University of Kentucky, and currently works as a technical editor in support of the aerospace industry. She resides in South Dakota with her husband and three children. Much of her work is inspired by nature which she explores on hiking adventures. Her poetry has been included in *Cholla Needles, Watershed, The Red Wheelbarrow, Noble Gas Quarterly, Pasque Petals* and *Oakwood Literary Magazine* which awarded her the 2017 Anita Bahr Award for Outstanding Contributor.

www.ingramcontent.com/pod-product-compliance
Lightning Source LLC
LaVergne TN
LVHW041602070426
835507LV00011B/1253